ANDY GLEADHILL'S

African Drumming Book 1

Published by:
Audible Music
PO BOX 2804
Bristol, BS6 9EQ
United Kingdom

www.andygleadhill.com

Andy Gleadhill's African Drumming
1.African Drumming, Music-instruction, and study
2. Ethnomusicology
3. Education

For Mary

ISBN 978-0957011502

Table of Contents

All tunes are traditional and arranged by Andy Gleadhill © 2007. All tunes were recorded using Drums for Schools instruments. MP3 recordings of each of the tunes can be downloaded from the relevant book product page on the Drums for Schools website, www.drumsforschools.co.uk. Video clips are also available - please visit the Drums for Schools You Tube channel.

Chapter
1

Introduction

The sound of African Drumming has captivated and inspired people for centuries. It is one of the earliest forms of communication and an important part of mankind's development. This book is aimed at helping students, teachers and African Drumming workshop leaders to enjoy playing a wide range of African rhythms and to be able to develop them into pieces of music ready for performance.

After this introduction we'll begin with some simple drumming warm-up exercises and an explanation of basic African Drumming techniques. Then we'll learn our first simple African beats and explain how to develop these rhythms into a performance-ready piece. Then follow ten African tunes with explanations of how they are played and suggestions on performance, including examples of Call and Response patterns.

Music in Africa

Music is an important part of life in Africa and fulfills many roles. Music is used in religious rituals, at ceremonies such as weddings, funerals and the birth of a child, as well as an accompaniment to day-to-day activities. There is music for working in the fields, tending cattle and collecting water as well as vastly contrasting music used for anything from lullabies to war songs. Everyone participates in music making and there is a wonderful saying that "In African music there is no audience, only participants". There are also professional musicians and master drummers who are highly valued. The use of music gives a cultural perspective to every aspect of daily life in Africa.

The prolific use of drums in African music demonstrates the importance of rhythm as the main ingredient in music making. African drumming is a language that can send messages, tell stories and communicate emotions. Drums in Africa come in many shapes and sizes and have many different playing styles. The drum has a high cultural status in Africa and there are many rituals that surround making, teaching and playing drums. When we play the African Drums and rhythms we are immersing ourselves in thousands of years of cultural and social history and sharing the universal joy of music making.

Chapter

1

Why the Djembe?

In this first African Drumming book I have written all the parts for the West African drum known as the Djembe. This is because the Djembe drum is simple to learn and yet is a versatile instrument, capable of producing a wide range of sounds. It is also reasonably priced and readily available.

Over the past twenty years the Djembe has experienced a meteoric rise in popularity both as the instrument of choice for hand drummers and as a souvenir for visitors to foreign lands.

Chapter

2

Basic Playing Techniques

The playing techniques of African Drums vary enormously across the African Continent with many different hand positions that not only change from country to country, but from village to village and each teacher may have a strongly held view as to how to play the drums "correctly". In my opinion there is no "correct" or standard method of playing African Drums but doing what comes naturally, with a little helpful advice, will result in a good clear tone. It is important that the Djembe Drums are played with the hands only and not with sticks, as sticks can easily damage the drum skin. To create the desired sounds and feel, the Djembe must be played with what I like to call a "Skin on Skin" technique. However, if you wish to practise the rhythms on a Drum Kit or Class Percussion then sticks may be used.

Playing position

To obtain the best tone and range of sounds from your drum it is essential that the Djembe is raised up from the ground and not played whilst it is standing on the floor. This is to allow the air and sound waves to escape from the bottom, open end of the drum. This is easily demonstrated by holding your hand against the open end of the drum while another player strikes the drum - you can feel the escaping air. It can also be demonstrated by leaving the drum on the floor and playing a few beats and then doing the same with the drum off the ground and noting the improvement in the sound from the dead tone with the drum on the floor to the rich ringing tone of the raised drum.

When considering the best playing position to adopt you need to take account of the ages of the performers, the size of the instruments they are using, as well as the numbers in the ensemble. Generally speaking my preferred playing position is with performers seated on the edge of a chair, to give more leg space for the drum, with backs straight and shoulders relaxed. The drum can then be placed between the thighs, just above the knee, and with the players feet crossed over on the floor around the drum. This will allow the player to have a firm grip on the drum and leave both hands free for playing.

Video example
How to play the Djembe drum

Producing the sounds

In this first book we will look at two basic Djembe sounds using different hand positions. They are the Open Tone and the Bass Tone.

The Open tone

This is the fundamental or rudimentary note of Djembe playing and it is important to master a good open tone on your instrument so you can play clear and even beats. When playing an open tone the drum should be struck with the whole length of the fingers on the edge of the drum nearest to your body with your elbows slightly raised. If you imagine the drumhead to be a clock face your right hand will be on the four and your left hand on the eight. Your hands must not remain in contact with the drum once you have played the beat but should return to your natural playing position just above the drum. A good way to achieve this technique is to imagine that the drumhead is very hot, like a radiator, and so you do not want to leave your hand on it any longer than necessary.

The Bass tone

A good Bass note will produce a full and rounded deep tone. This is one of the sounds that are characteristic of the Djembe and its hourglass shape. To produce a good Bass tone the Djembe must be struck in the middle of the drumhead with the hand slightly cupped, palm down, again with the hand returning quickly from the drum. You can use your whole arm and pretend that you are bouncing a basketball and this will result in the correct action for playing good Bass tones.

In the grid music notation used later in this book the Open Tone is written with a capital **H** to represent its High sound and the Bass Tone is represented with the letter **L** for its Low sound.

Group Playing

Although it is possible to play African Drums as solo instruments, it is more commonly seen as a group activity. Making music and having fun while interacting with other musicians is all part of the African Drumming experience, hence the saying that in African music there is no audience, only participants! It is a good idea that everyone who is present joins in with the music, if only by clapping along.

Chapter

2

Setting up the room

The layout of the room that your group is using will make all the difference to the sound of the ensemble. In this book most of the African rhythms are written out in three parts. This is to represent the three different sizes of drums that I recommend are used and are set out in the music as follows.

1. Large Djembe Drums
2. Medium Djembe Drums
3. Small Djembe Drums

It is important that each part of the music is equally balanced and not drowned out by another part. If you have a large number of the big Bass drums and only a few small drums you will not achieve a balanced sound. The larger drums by nature will have a bigger sound than the smaller ones so you may only need a few big drums and more medium and small drums to create an overall balanced sound.

I suggest that the musicians are arranged in a semi-circle with the largest drums on the left, the medium drums in the middle and the small drums to the right with the teacher or leader sitting opposite the semicircle facing the middle players.

Positioning diagram

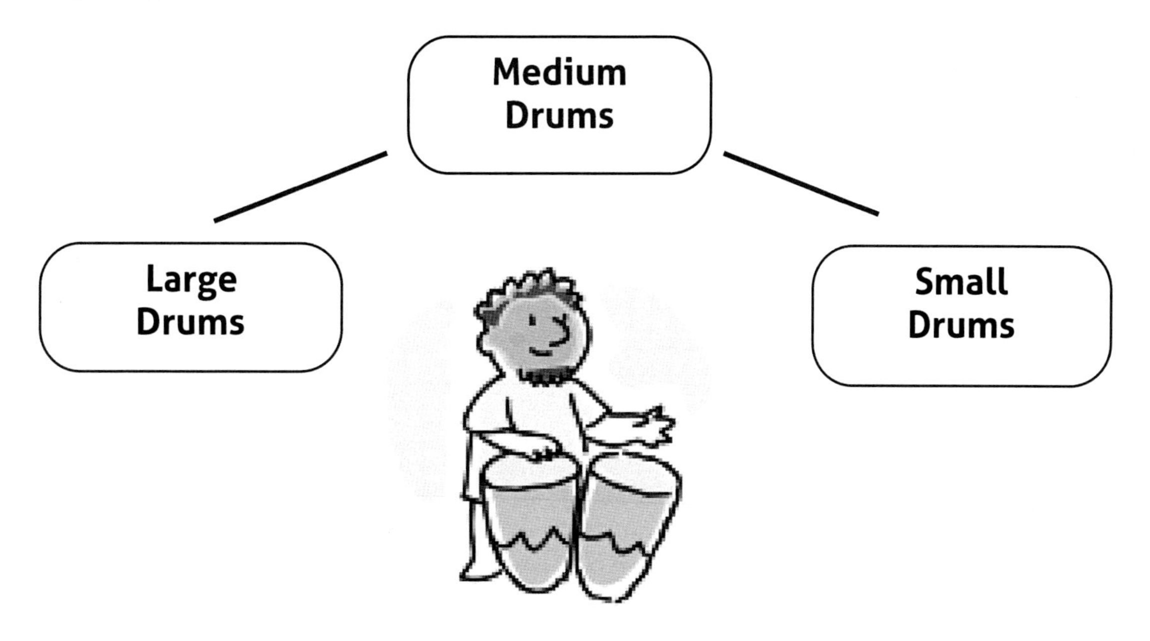

Chapter

3

Grid Music

The music grid is an easy way to learn the African rhythms without having to read western musical notation. The grid is made up of horizontal lines and vertical columns.
The top shaded line of the Grid indicates the beat number. These run evenly from beat one to beat sixteen or to twelve in tunes Madagascar and M'baba.

Here is a blank 16 beat grid:

1	2	3	4

5	6	7	8

9	10	11	12

13	14	15	16

In the examples and tunes that follow throughout the book, there may be different grids for the different parts: Drums One, Drums Two and Drums Three . These correspond to the different size and pitches of the drums as described in the section on group playing.

Each drum plays either a high or open tone when the letter "H" appears under the beat number or a low or Bass tone when the letter "L" appears under the beat number. The letter "O" indicates a rest when the drum plays no sound.

Each rhythm loops round and round so after beat sixteen, we immediately start again at beat one, though in practise it is easier to count the beats in groups of four, rather than from one to sixteen.

The grid is made up of horizontal lines and vertical columns.

The name of each instrument is written next to its individual part.

The top shaded line of the Grid indicates the beat number.

These run evenly from beat one to beat sixteen.

This makes it easier to see each group of four beats when practising and learning the rhythms.

When playing and performing the whole piece there should be no gaps between the beats and the rhythms should flow evenly through all the beat numbers.

Chapter 3

Here is an example of a music grid playing four high tones followed by four low tones.

.

Medium Djembes

1	2	3	4
H	O	H	O

5	6	7	8
H	O	H	O

9	10	11	12
L	O	L	O

13	14	15	16
L	O	L	O

However, in the warm up exercises we will use the letters **R** and **L** in upper case to indicate that the drum should be struck with either the right or left hand.

So the key to the music is as follows:

In the warm up exercises:

R = Play with the Right Hand
L = Play with the Left Hand
Sh = Play a Short Note
tr = Play a Long Note or Roll

In the ten African tunes:

H = Play a High Sound with an Open Tone
L = Play a Low Sound with a Bass Tone
U = Play with both hands at the same time (unison)
O = A rest or silent beat when no sound is played
W = Play the Whistle
tr = Play a Long Note or Roll

For information about basic playing techniques and producing the sounds please refer to Chapter 2: Basic Playing Techniques.

Chapter

3

Elements of Music

African Drumming is an excellent way to learn about music as it incorporates all the basic elements of music into a lesson from the very beginning.

Below is a list of the basic elements of music. I will identify where they are introduced in the warm up exercises that follow in the next chapter.

Whenever you are playing the African Drums, see if you can recognise the elements of music that you are using.

1 **Rhythm** .... A beat or pulse

2 **Tempo** ....The speed of the music e.g. slow or fast

3 **Pitch** ....High and low sounds

4 **Dynamics** .... Loud and soft sounds

5 **Duration**..................................Short and long sounds

6 **Timbre** ....The different "colour" or sound of each instrument

7 **Texture** ....Thick and thin sounds of many or solo players

8 **Structure** ....The way a tune is put together

Warm-up Exercises

Warm-ups

When playing African Drums, as with any other instrument, it is important that the group warms up before starting to play the African tunes. Just as an athlete would not go into a race cold the African Drummer needs to do some exercises to prepare their muscles before playing the tunes. Here are some simple drumming exercises that will develop co-ordination and a sense of pulse that I suggest begins every session with your African Drumming Group.
First of all become focused and prepare for the session by trying to relax and loosen any tension by letting your arms flop loosely to your sides and gently shake and relax your arms and shoulders. Try the same with each leg in turn. Gently roll your head in a circle, then take deep breaths and release slowly.

We can now start to play the warm up exercises below. Each exercise has the numbers for the elements of music that it employs.

Exercise One - Rhythm

1a. R L R L R L R L (R=right hand and L=left hand)

The purpose of this exercise is to establish a steady and even beat.**(Element 1, Rhythm)**

Play even beats one hand after the other, called single strokes, using using the Open Tone technique described in Chapter 2.

To start with the leader can play the first four beats with the group answering by playing the second group of four beats straight after.

1	2	3	4
R	L	R	L

5	6	7	8
R	L	R	L

9	10	11	12
R	L	R	L

13	14	15	16
R	L	R	L

Please note, in all warm ups L = Play with the left hand and R = play with the Right hand.

Remember to start steadily with a good even pulse like a clock ticking (clock ticks are equal to 120 beats per minute -120 BPM). There will be a natural tendency to speed up so you must concentrate on keeping the beat steady and not rushing.

Tempo and Pulse (Elements 1 and 2, Rhythm and Tempo)

When the group is able to maintain a good steady beat (this may be after a few weeks of rehearsals) try alternating between the normal tempo and half speed, then back to normal tempo and then double speed, with the underlying pulse always remaining the same.

This will sound and be played like this:

Normal speed

1	2	3	4	5	6	7	8	9	10	11	12	13	14	15	16
R	L	R	L	R	L	R	L	R	L	R	L	R	L	R	L

Half speed

1	2	3	4	5	6	7	8	9	10	11	12	13	14	15	16
R	O	L	O	R	O	L	O	R	O	L	O	R	O	L	O

Normal speed

1	2	3	4	5	6	7	8	9	10	11	12	13	14	15	16
R	L	R	L	R	L	R	L	R	L	R	L	R	L	R	L

Double speed

1	2	3	4	5	6	7	8	9	10	11	12	13	14	15	16
rl	rl	rl	rl	rl	rl	rl	rl	rl	rl	rl	rl	rl	rl	rl	rl

1b. R R L L R R L L

This exercise now uses two beats to each hand or double strokes and can be performed in the same ways as exercise 1a at normal, half and double speeds.

1	2	3	4	5	6	7	8	9	10	11	12	13	14	15	16
R	R	L	L	R	R	L	L	R	R	L	L	R	R	L	L

1c. R L R R L R L L

This exercise has jumbled up single and double strokes and is known as a Paradiddle and again, it can be performed using the same techniques as in exercise 1a, alternating between normal, half and double speeds. (Element 2 Tempo)

1	2	3	4	5	6	7	8	9	10	11	12	13	14	15	16
R	L	R	R	L	R	L	L	R	L	R	R	L	R	L	L

Players who are left-handed may prefer to start with their left hand. This is perfectly acceptable and will be a mirror image of the above exercises. i.e.

1a. L R L R L R L R 1b. L L R R L L R R 1c. L R L L R L R R

Video example
African_Drumming_Warm_Up_Exercises..m4v

Exercise Two – Highs and Lows

(Elements 1, 2 and 3, Rhythm, Tempo and Pitch)

For these warm up exercises we will need to use two different playing techniques to create a High and Low sound (see "Producing the Sounds" in Chapter 2: Basic Playing Techniques).

2a. Four Highs and four Lows

We are now adding in musical element 3, pitch into our warm ups by playing four High tones followed by four Low tones.

H= High sound **L**= Low sound.

This exercise can be performed using the same playing techniques as 1a.

1	2	3	4	5	6	7	8	9	10	11	12	13	14	15	16
H	H	H	H	L	L	L	L	H	H	H	H	L	L	L	L

2b. Two Lows and two Highs

Again we can play this in the same manner as 1b.

1	2	3	4	5	6	7	8	9	10	11	12	13	14	15	16
H	H	L	L	H	H	L	L	H	H	L	L	H	H	L	L

2c. again as 1c, but with the combination of Low and High tones.

1	2	3	4	5	6	7	8	9	10	11	12	13	14	15	16
H	L	H	H	L	H	L	L	H	L	H	H	L	H	L	L

Don't forget you can also try exercises 2a, 2b, and 2c, using the different speeds as explained in the pulse section.

Exercise Three – Short and Long sounds

3a. Short, short, long (Element 5 Duration)

This exercise introduces the musical element of **Duration** or length of note.
Here we will play two short notes in the normal way that we played single beats in exercise 1a, followed by one longer note that will be played as a Roll.

First it is a good idea to practise just the long note or Roll. A Roll is performed by the drummer playing one hand after the other as fast as possible. Try to keep your Roll even by using each hand with equal weight and speed. When you are happy with your Roll you can play exercise 3a. Make sure your long note (Roll) is equal in length to the previous two short notes (and lasts 4 beats of the pulse).

1	2	3	4	5	6	7	8	9	10	11	12	13	14	15	16
Sh	O	Sh	O	L tr	O tr	N tr	G tr	Sh	O	Sh	O	L tr	O tr	N tr	G tr

3b. Long, short, short (Elements 1, 3 and 5 , Pitch and Duration)

This is the reverse of 3a, with the long note being played first.

1	2	3	4	5	6	7	8	9	10	11	12	13	14	15	16
L tr	O tr	N tr	G tr	Sh	O	Sh	O	L tr	O tr	N tr	G tr	Sh	O	Sh	G

When the group have mastered this exercise try playing the first long note on a high sound on the edge or rim of the drum and the following two short notes on a low tone in the centre of the drum skin (see “producing the sounds in Chapter 2, Basic Playing Techniques).

3c. Combined

(Elements 1, 3,4,5,6 and 8 Rhythm, Pitch, Dynamics, Duration, Timbre and Structure)

Now we will need to divide the group into two halves. The side to the leader's left will play exercise 3a, and the side to the right will play 3b. Both groups will start playing at the same time. Ask each group to play their short notes softly and their long notes loudly and to listen to the sound of the long note as it moves from one side of the room to the other.

3d. Combined, with highs and lows (Elements 1,2,3,4,5,6,7 and 8 Rhythm, Tempo, Pitch, Dynamics, Duration, Timbre Texture and Structure)

Now we will ask the left side of the group to play exercise 3a, with the short notes played softly on the edge of their instruments and the right side of the group will play exercise 3b, starting with a loud, long note played on with a low note on the centre of the drum head.

When you have established a steady rhythm swap between normal, half and double tempos as before, also ask just one player on each side to play the long note to vary the texture of the music.

This last exercise combines all the elements of music we have explored so far.

Chapter

4

Exercise Four – Repeat after me

4a, This is a simple selection of easy, four beat phrases, which the group can repeat straight after being played by the leader.
When you are confident with these try making up your own rhythms for the others to repeat.
Members of the group can also take it in terns to make up rhythms for everyone to repeat.

Leader / Group

1	2	3	4	5	6	7	8	9	10	11	12	13	14	15	16
H	O	L	O	L	L	L	O	H	O	L	O	L	L	L	O

Leader / Group

1	2	3	4	5	6	7	8	9	10	11	12	13	14	15	16
H	H	H	O	L	L	L	O	H	H	H	O	L	L	L	O

Leader / Group

1	2	3	4	5	6	7	8	9	10	11	12	13	14	15	16
H	H	O	L	H	O	H	O	H	H	O	L	H	O	H	O

Leader / Group

1	2	3	4	5	6	7	8	9	10	11	12	13	14	15	16
H	O	L	L	O	H	H	O	H	O	L	L	O	H	H	O

When the group is confident with this format try experimenting with different combinations of high and low sounds, or scratch the drumhead or clap your hands instead.
See how creative you can be!

Chapter

5

Call and Response

Call and Response patterns (sometimes referred to as Questions and Answers) are an integral part and a key characteristic of African Music.

Listen to any African Music, particularly vocal music and you will notice that it is filled with examples of Call and Response, often with a vocal solo being answered by a response from the chorus. Call and Response patterns are also a common part of communication in the natural world. Animal calls, football chants and even political speeches (the addresses of Martin Luther King are a good example), are all punctuated with calls and responses.

African Drumming can be seen as a conversation between different drums with Call and Response patterns being a dialogue between the leader and the rest of the group.

Call and Responses often mark transitions in the music and can be used to link one African rhythm to another.

The ideal Call and Response should slip seamlessly in and out of the African tune that is being played - see lesson five in Chapter 7.

There are many variations of Call and Response patterns, two of which we will use in this first book: A Rhythm to Repeat and A Rhythm to Respond to.

Chapter

5

A Rhythm to Repeat

This is the simplest of Call and Responses , in which a rhythm is played by the leader and then repeated by the whole group.
Any of the examples given in the “repeat after me” section of the Warm up Chapter can be used.
You should also have a go at making up your own.

A Rhythm to Respond to

These are Call and Response patterns where the answering phrases are different to the initial calls.
I have written out three easy examples below in grid musical notation.
In the first two examples (1a and 1b) the call is played by the leader and the response by the group. In example 2a we use a whistle (Apito), marked by "w" in the grid, to play the call and the whole group play the response.
The use of a whistle is helpful as the group can hear it above the drumming and it gives the group time to prepare to play the response.

Using Words and Phrases

The Call and Response patterns can be taught using words and phrases, which fit with the rhythms of the music.
I have written out some examples for Call and Responses 1a, 1b and 2a but have left 2b blank, as it is also fun to make up your own!

1A

Call

1	2	3	4	5	6	7	8	9	10	11	12	13	14	15	16
we	o	want	o	you	o	o	o	we	o	want	o	you	o	o	o

Response

1	2	3	4	5	6	7	8	9	10	11	12	13	14	15	16
we	o	want	o	you	as	o	a	new	o	re	o	crut	o	o	o

Chapter 5

1B

Call / Response

1	2	3	4	5	6	7	8	9	10	11	12	13	14	15	16
I	o	told	a	joke	o	go	o	o	o	boom	o	boom	o	o	o

2A

Call / Response

1	2	3	4	5	6	7	8	9	10	11	12	13	14	15	16
w	-	-	-	w	-	-	-	eat	ing	o	ba	na	o	nas	o

Call / Response

1	2	3	4	5	6	7	8	9	10	11	12	13	14	15	16
w	-	-	-	w	-	-	-	gives	o	you	o	en	er	gy	o

2B

1	2	3	4	5	6	7	8	9	10	11	12	13	14	15	16

1	2	3	4	5	6	7	8	9	10	11	12	13	14	15	16

Chapter

6

Percussion Buddies

How does Percussion Buddies for African Drumming work?

The concept is very simple: at the outset the class is divided up into pairs of "Buddies". The pairs take it in turn to play the main instrument, in this case the djembe, whilst the one not playing the main instrument is the **"Percussion Buddy"** and plays one of the African percussion instruments in an accompanying role . The Buddies exchange instruments several times during a lesson so that in each lesson both pupils have time playing both the main instrument and the percussion instrument and the point is that everyone is actively engaged throughout – there's no "waiting for my turn". The Buddy pairs can be the same for each lesson or pupils can change buddies from lesson to lesson at the discretion of the teacher.

The **Percussion Buddies** approach allows teachers and schools to carry out really effective whole class instrumental teaching even with very limited resources. If there are not enough main instruments for all pupils, then regardless of the instrument or musical style that is being taught, **"Percussion Buddies"** will help you to engage and involve all of the pupils all of the time. The Percussion Buddy approach will enable every pupil to participate fully and meaningfully throughout the lesson and at the same time learn notation skills and all the elements of music. This will also help drumming groups, particularly Djembe and other African Drumming Groups to expand the number of players in the group by adding additional African Percussion instruments to their ensemble.

A further benefit is that the approach enables the group to develop a much wider range of musical colours or timbres (see Elements of Music, page 6) to their sound and allows more participation from players of any musical ability.

Below I will describe three popular African Percussion instruments and explain how they should be played. I'll then suggest some rhythmic patterns that the instruments can play for some popular African tunes.

The African Percussion instruments we shall be using are:
The Natural Agogos (but you can use metal agogos or any 2 tone percussion instrument)
The Caxixi Shaker
The Seseh Shaker (Beaded Cabasa Shaker)

Chapter 6

Here is a description of each instrument:

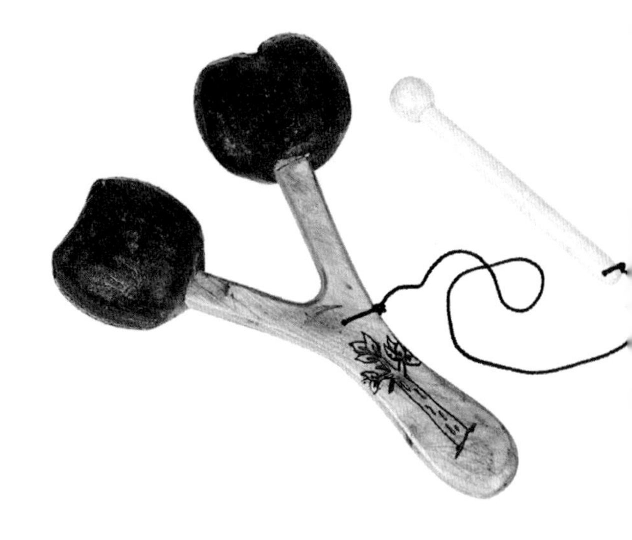

The Natural Agogos

Originally these instruments were fashioned from the bells attached to cattle and goats that would sound as the animal moved so that the worker tending the animals was able to locate them in dense bush. They consist of one high pitched and one low pitched palm shell. They are modeled on African metal bells and Latin American Agogo Bells which are an integral part of Brazilian Samba Music.

The Caxixi

Resembling a small basket, this instrument is a woven from rattan or reeds and is formed in a conical shape with the larger end sealed by a circular piece of gourd and the smaller end tapering to a short handle. The basket is filled with beads or seeds to create the shaker sounds. It can be made in different sizes from small to large.

The Seseh Shaker (Beaded Cabasa Shaker)

This instrument is fashioned from a gourd or coconut which has bean covered with a net of beads. It has a handle for holding the instrument. To create the sounds the gourd can be tapped, shaken or twisted. It is often used as an accompaniment to music for dancing. There are may variants of this instrument - cabasa shakers, beaded shakers to name but two.

Chapter

6

How to play the Buddy Instruments

A word about Percussion

All three instruments are percussion instruments. Percussion instruments are defined as ones that are played by being plucked, shaken, struck with sticks, hands or other parts of the body. The skills and techniques used by percussionists (musicians who play percussion instruments) are often concentrated around producing as wide a variety of sounds as possible from the instruments. Percussionists also work on creating sustained sounds from instruments that normally have short sounds and creating short sounds from instruments that have long, sustained sounds.

The Natural Agogos

Playing position

The Natural Agogos should be held in one hand with the arm stretched out in front of the player with the beater held in the other hand.

Producing the sounds

This instrument has two palm shells. one that will produce a high pitched sound and the other a lower sound. First play both palm shells to find out which plays the higher and which plays the lower sound. By alternating between the high and low sounds the player can produce lots of interesting rhythms. Grip the stick between the pad of the thumb and the first joint of the index finger. The wrist should be turned inwards with the palm facing downwards. The stick should be held towards the bottom end of the shaft with the fingers curled in a row along the stick. Try to leave some of the bottom end of the shaft protruding from your palm to create a good balance and so the ball end of the beater is not top heavy. Keep your elbow slightly raised up and away from your body. When you strike the instrument try to keep your forearm still and move your wrist as if you are flicking a drop of water from the end of the beater.

Natural Agogo

1	2	3	4
L	O	H	O

In the grid music the Natural Agogos are played with a low sound when the letter L appears in the cell and a high sound when the letter H appears.

The Caxixi

Playing position

The Caxixi should be held in your hand in a horizontal position with the flat bottom of the instrument facing to the left if held in your right hand or to the right if held in the left hand.

The Caxixi are best played from a standing position with the instrument held in your dominant hand with your elbow bent and your forearm in a vertical or upright position with the palm of your hand holding the instrument facing you.

Producing the sounds

From the playing position described above rock the instrument forwards and then backwards away and towards your body to create a steady beat. The first movement away from your body should be to a high position. You can twist your wrist so that the leather end of the instrument faces away from you to produce a different accented tone. This action should be as if throwing a dart.

In the grid music the letter F in the cell indicates when the instrument is played in a forward motion and the letter B when it is in a backward motion. The letter X indicates and accent when the wrist is twisted so the beads inside the instrument strike the hard base of the Caxixi as explained above. The letter O indicates a rest when no sound is played. See the example below.

Caxixi

1	2	3	4
F	B	F	X

Chapter

6

Seseh Shaker (Beaded Cabasa Shaker)

Playing position

The Seseh Shaker can be played in a similar way to the Maracas, shaken back and forth in a rhythmic fashion or played into the open palm of the opposite hand to produce short beats. It can also be twisted from side to side to produce a sustained roll in the same way as a Tambourine.

Producing the sounds

As well as shaking the instrument you can tap it with your fingers to produce different rhythms. Also try holding your free hand against the beads and twisting the wrist of your other hand holding the handle. This will create short or longer sounds.

In the grid music the letter F in the cell indicates when the instrument is played in a forward motion and the letter B when it is in a backward motion. The letter T indicates when the wrist is twisted so the beads on the instrument move across the body of the Shaker as explained above. The letter O indicates a rest when no sound is played. See the example below.

Beaded Shaker

1	2	3	4
F	B	F	T

How percussion buddies fit in with the music of the whole group

Members of the class or group should "Buddy up" in pairs - some classes may already be used to doing this for other activities such as sport or reading. Buddies will literally sit or stand next to each other, one with the main instrument of the whole class lesson (the djembe in this case) and the other with the percussion instrument.

In the following pages there are examples of patterns rhythms and percussion music that the percussion buddy can play along side whatever music is being played by the main instrument. As this is aimed at first access initial introduction to music, the examples are kept to simple rhythms in basic time signatures. There are also some blank grids for you to experiment with.

The percussion players should make sure that they play with the same dynamics (volumes) and tempos (speeds) as the other instrumentalists.

If the tune is very fast and the percussion players are not able physically to play at the quicker tempo, then their parts can be played at half speed (and vice versa if the tempo is it is a very slow tune).

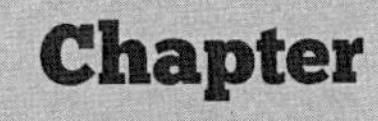

Percussion Buddies score for African drumming tunes in 4/4 e.g. Sogo, Polole, Koukou, Jongo, Bowra, D'jole, Fanga

Natural Agogos

1	2	3	4	5	6	7	8	9	10	11	12	13	14	15	16
H	O	L	O	H	H	L	O	H	O	L	O	H	H	L	O

Caxixi

1	2	3	4	5	6	7	8	9	10	11	12	13	14	15	16
F	B	F	B	F	B	F	X	F	B	F	B	F	B	F	X

Seseh Shaker

1	2	3	4	5	6	7	8	9	10	11	12	13	14	15	16
F	B	F	T	F	B	F	T	F	B	F	T	F	B	F	T

Natural Agogos

1	2	3	4	5	6	7	8	9	10	11	12	13	14	15	16

Caxixi

1	2	3	4	5	6	7	8	9	10	11	12	13	14	15	16

Seseh Shaker

1	2	3	4	5	6	7	8	9	10	11	12	13	14	15	16

Chapter

6

Percussion Buddies score for African drumming tunes in 3 time

Natural Agogos

1	2	3
H	O	O

1	2	3
L	O	O

1	2	3
H	O	L

1	2	3
H	O	O

Caxixi

1	2	3
F	O	B

1	2	3
F	O	B

1	2	3
F	B	X

1	2	3
F	O	O

Seseh Shaker

1	2	3
F	O	B

1	2	3
F	O	B

1	2	3
F	O	T

1	2	3
F	O	O

Natural Agogos

1	2	3

1	2	3

1	2	3

1	2	3

Caxixi

1	2	3

1	2	3

1	2	3

1	2	3

Seseh Shaker

1	2	3

1	2	3

1	2	3

1	2	3

Chapter 6

Percussion Buddies score for African drumming tunes in 6 time e.g. M'baba

Natural Agogos

1	2	3	4	5	6
H	O	L	H	O	O

Caxixi

1	2	3	4	5	6
F	O	B	X	O	O

Seseh Shaker

1	2	3	4	5	6
F	O	B	F	T	O

Natural Agogos

1	2	3	4	5	6

Caxixi

1	2	3	4	5	6

Seseh Shaker

1	2	3	4	5	6

Chapter

6

Percussion Buddies score for African drumming tunes in 12 time e.g. Madagascar

Natural Agogos

1	2	3	4	5	6
H	O	O	L	O	O

1	2	3	4	5	6
H	O	L	H	O	O

Caxixi

1	2	3	4	5	6
F	B	F	X	O	O

1	2	3	4	5	6
F	B	F	X	O	O

Seseh Shaker

1	2	3	4	5	6
F	B	F	T	O	O

1	2	3	4	5	6
T	O	O	T	O	O

Natural Agogos

1	2	3	4	5	6

1	2	3	4	5	6

Caxixi

1	2	3	4	5	6

1	2	3	4	5	6

Seseh Shaker

1	2	3	4	5	6

1	2	3	4	5	6

Percussion Buddies score for African drumming tunes in fast 2 time e.g. The Conga

Natural Agogos

1	2	1	2	1	2	1	2
H	O	L	O	H	H	L	O

Caxixi

1	2	1	2	1	2	1	2
F	B	F	B	X	B	F	B

Seseh Shaker

1	2	1	2	1	2	1	2
F	B	F	B	F	B	T	O

Natural Agogos

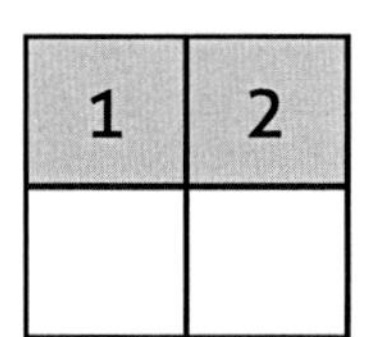

1	2	1	2	1	2	1	2

Caxixi

1	2	1	2	1	2	1	2

Seseh Shaker

1	2	1	2	1	2	1	2

Chapter

7

Lesson Plans

A well-structured lesson will ensure that an individual or group can achieve the best results from their time playing African drums. First I'm going to suggest a structure for a standard 40-minute lesson and then I'll go on to propose a scheme of 10 lessons for a group of beginners.

Objectives

The objectives of an African Drumming lesson could be summarised as follows:

- To learn to play the drums musically, with good time keeping and solid, steady rhythm.
- To understand, identify and use all the Elements of Music.
- To understand the history and social context of African Drumming.
- To be able to play a range of African rhythms in a variety of styles.
- To be able to use these skills to play as a member of a group, interacting with other players and employing listening and improvisation skills.

Outcomes

After playing with an African drumming group pupils will be able to:

- Maintain a steady rhythm.
- Play and recognise a range of different African rhythms.
- Show improved listening skills and be able to play as a member of a performing ensemble,
- React to Call and Response patterns and follow directions from a lead player.

Chapter 7

General Lesson Structure (but see following notes for lessons 1 to 3)

Warm ups
As described in Chapter 2 (10 minutes)

First tune
An easy tune that the group is familiar with or, if this is the first lesson, begin to learn The Conga. You can find The Conga grids and teaching and learning notes on page 60 of this book. (5 minutes)

Develop the tune
Start to give the tune some structure as described in the weekly lesson notes (5 minutes)

Add some Call and Response
Start to introduce an appropriate Call and Response pattern as described in the lesson notes and Chapter 5 (5 minutes)

Work on new material
Introduce some new material. Work on a new, more advanced tune from the book as "work in progress". All tunes in this book are graduated so that each new tune is slightly more advanced and introduces more musical challenges than the previous one. (10 minutes)

Performance
Try to end the lesson by pulling together the music you have been working on and play it through as a performance. See Chapter 8 Creating a Performance. (5 minutes)

Chapter

7

Ten Weekly Lessons

Week One

It is important that the first lesson is spent getting to know the instruments and becoming comfortable with the playing position. Demonstrating the way that the air flows through the drum will help students to understand why the drum needs to be held off the ground. This is described in the paragraph on "playing position" in Chapter 1.

Talking about the music of Africa will help to give some historical and social context to the lessons, as explained in the introduction.

Of course students will want to play as soon as possible so begin by explaining the playing technique for the open tone and play warm up exercise number 1a. Explain the meaning of the letters R and L and concentrate on maintaining a steady beat with even sounds.

If the group is ready you can introduce exercise 1b and 1c.

Each lesson from now on can begin with these three exercises and each week we will aim to improve the quality of the sound whilst achieving good steady beats.

End this lesson by trying some of the "repeat after me" examples in Chapter 4 exercise 4a. Make sure each member of the group tries a different size drum each week and remember to use the Percussion Buddy method from Chapter 6 to involve all the learners.

Week Two

Begin with a revision of the previous week's warm ups. For the first three weeks of drumming the students may only need to work on playing the warm up exercises and developing good hand positioning on the drums. In the second week we can introduce high and low sounds.

Explain the technique for producing the Bass tone on the drum and the meaning of the letters H and L in the music. Again, concentrate on the quality of the sounds being produced as well as working on playing together as a group.

At the end of the lesson try some more of the "repeat after me" examples and each week the accuracy of the replies will improve.

Chapter 7

Week Three

The lesson will naturally begin with warm up exercises 1a, b and c.

This is now a good time to introduce tempo and pulse, element 2, to the exercises as explained in Chapter 3.

Now try exercises 2a, b and c along with the tempo changes as before.

We can now move on to exercises 3a, b, c and d, which will introduce element 5, duration. Play these exercises as explained in Chapter 4.

To finish this lesson play the "repeat after me" exercises once more and then try improvising your own rhythms as explained in exercise 4b.

Week Four

From now on it will be possible to follow the lesson structure from the earlier part of this chapter.

Begin with the entire warm up exercises, which, by now, the students will be familiar with (lesson structure part 1). We now only need to spend around five minutes on these exercises.

The tune we will look at to teach in this chapter is tune nine, "The Conga." Relate this to the group using the music and teaching and learning notes in Chapter 9, page 60. To begin with the teacher or leader can play the first four-note or "Everybody" part and the rest of the group will answer with the two- note "Conga".

When this is satisfactory split the group in two and ask the left hand side with the larger drums to play the four-note part and the right hand side with the smaller drums to play the two-note part.

Now we can add in some pitch by asking the larger drums on the right hand side to play their part using the playing technique to produce the Bass tone and the smaller drums to use an open tone.

End the lesson with some more "repeat after me" patterns.

Chapter

7

Week Five

Following the general lesson structure, we begin with the entire warm up procedure.

We then recap the work on The Conga from the previous lesson.

This can now be developed by teaching the students to play both parts of The Conga on their drums by playing the four-note "everybody" part in the centre of their drum using the Bass tone playing technique, followed by the "conga" part on the edge of the drum using the open tone technique.

The Call and Response pattern that works best with The Conga is 2a, "eating bananas". First learn the call "eating bananas" on its own, playing the rhythm after two blasts on the whistle.

Next try practising playing the "gives you energy" rhythm in the same way. Now play the entire Call and Response pattern.

As mentioned in Chapter 5, Call and Response patterns need to fit into our African rhythms without any interruption to the flow of the beat or the pulse of the music. To begin to practise this, go back to playing The Conga with the teacher or leader only playing the four-beat "everybody" part and with the rest of the group responding with the two-beat "conga" part. Now, at any time, the leader can play the two blasts on the whistle instead of the four-note part and the group can respond with "eating bananas" followed by two more whistles and the response "gives you energy" as written out in the musical example 2A. This phrase should be repeated twice and at the end of the second "gives you energy" the leader can revert to playing their four-beat "everybody" rhythm with the group carrying on with the two-beat "conga".

This will take some time to perfect so remember to practise slowly at first and gradually increase the tempo as the group become more confident.

End the lesson as before with some more "repeat after me" patterns.

Chapter 7

Week Six

Begin the lesson as before following the general lesson structure.

To develop The Conga further, try to link together the different ways that The Conga has been played in previous weeks using the call and response 2A as a link between the sections.

This will start to build the separate parts into a performance-ready piece.

The first section is performed with the leader playing the four-beat "everybody" part and the rest of the group playing the two-beat "conga".

The second section has the larger drums on the right hand side playing the four-beat "everybody" part and the smaller drums on the left playing the two-beat "conga".

The third section is performed with the whole group playing both parts - the four-beat "everybody" played in the centre of the drum using the Bass tone and the two-beat "conga" as an open tone at the edge of the drum. Each section can be linked with Call and Response 2A.

Week Seven

After the warm up procedure, practise the three sections of The Conga, which the students were taught in previous lessons.

Now practise linking the sections with Call and Response 2A.

Return to the third section of The Conga, playing the four-beat "everybody" part in the centre of the drum using the Bass tone one hand after the other (e.g. R L R L) and the two-beat "conga" part on the edge of the drum using both hands together at the same time (known as unison and sometimes written with the letter U). From now on always try to perform the third section only in this way.

Week Eight

When the group has warmed up and revised the three sections of The Conga try learning Call and Response 1B. This will be used to end your performance. practise it slowly at first and gradually increase the tempo at which you perform it. In the actual performance you can play this last Call and Response as fast as you can comfortably play it!

Chapter 7

Now go back to the third section of The Conga and try playing it first with only the leader playing the phrase "everybody conga, c'mon and do The Conga". The leader repeats this phrase twice as a solo and after the second time is joined by the next player in the semi-circle - again for two phrases - and so on until the entire group is playing. Remember to play the third section using one hand after the other for the four-beats and both hands together (unison) for the two-beat parts.

Week Nine

After the warm ups this lesson (and any other remaining lessons) can be dedicated to practising the completed performance as follows.

The performance can begin with the leader only playing the four-beat "everybody" part and the group playing the two-beat "conga". Continue playing this section round and round for about 30 seconds.

Next seamlessly slip into the Call and Response 2A. After the second "gives you energy", the larger drums on the right hand side of the group immediately take over the four-beat "everybody" part with the smaller drums on the left playing the two-beat "conga". After playing this version for a while add in the Call and Response 2A for another time.

As before, after the second "gives you energy" ,the leader only plays both parts of The Conga, using the Bass and open tones as described in lesson five. After the leader has played the "everybody conga, c'mon and do The Conga" pattern twice on their own, the next player in the semi-circle joins in and then each player in turn until the whole group are playing. Once the entire group are playing in unison the leader can gradually increase the speed of the music until it becomes too fast to play and the rhythm dissolves into a long roll. The leader will then raise their hands to signal to the group to stop playing and the performance will end with Call and Response 1B played at a fast tempo four times. Listen to the mp3 track to hear a complete performance.

Week Ten - The Performance

This is what you have been working towards during your lessons so try to make your performance as much of an event and exciting as possible. Invite classmates, parents, friends, anyone you can think of to share your African drumming experience. Dress up in traditional African style clothes, prepare some African food to share. Music is meant to be shared so enjoy celebrating your achievements. Refer to the next Chapter, Creating a Performance, for ideas and suggestions for making this a lesson to remember.

Chapter

8

Creating a Performance

All the musical examples in this book are short representations of original beats and rhythms from all over Africa. In this chapter we will look at ways that we can develop and expand the rhythms into performance-ready pieces. An example of building a performance out of a simple African rhythm is described in the weekly lesson guide in Chapter 7. As with any good song or piece of music it is important to have a solid structure.

A template for developing our African rhythms into performance ready pieces can be described as follows:

1. **Introduction**
2. **Establishing the rhythm**
3. **Adding a Call and Response**
4. **Developing the rhythm**
5. **Conclusion and ending**

Introduction

The beginning of a piece of music will have an effect on the rest of the performance so it is important that the music gets off to a good start.

It is sometimes said that all good musical performances begin with silence, but this is not always possible and sometimes the music needs to begin with some dramatic, attention-seeking statement.

Sometimes the music can begin using one of the Call and Response patterns as a link into the first rhythm. Playing fast rolls that begin softly and then crescendo into a loud mass of sound can be an effective way of opening a performance. Even one of the warm up exercises can be used as an introduction to any of the African beats.

Establishing the rhythm

Whichever African rhythm you are performing, establishing a good steady rhythm, after the introduction, will create a good foundation for what follows.

When establishing the rhythm at the beginning, it is a good idea to keep it to its simplest form and save the more complicated variations for later in the performance.

Chapter

8

Adding a Call and Response

Once the basic rhythm has been established and played round and round a number of times a Call and Response pattern can be introduced from the list of suitable patterns or one you have composed yourself. The Call and Response patterns can be used to link together different variations of each African rhythm. In extended performances Call and Response patterns can also be used as a bridge between different African rhythms.

Developing the rhythm

To make the performances more interesting, two or three different variations of each African rhythm can be incorporated into the performance. Try playing each part of the rhythm on different size drums and experiment with swapping the parts between the different sizes.

Dividing the group into two with each side taking it in turns to play the tune, will create an interesting stereo effect. Some of the African rhythms will work as a "round", with groups of players starting the rhythm at different times, e.g. have a second group start again after 4 beats. Using dynamics (loud and soft volumes) can also be used to dramatic effect.

When the group has become confident and familiar with the rhythms, individual group members can take turns to improvise and solo on top of the established rhythm. Try to keep each solo reasonably short and in the same style as the underlying beat. Rhythmic patterns that are used in the original beat can be rearranged and incorporated into a solo. Improvisation is a skill that will take time to become comfortable with so try to practise it regularly.

Conclusion and ending

As with the introduction, the ending of a performance needs to be well worked out in advance and to be musically tight and tidy. Some of the Call and Response patterns work well as an ending, particularly if it is not one you have used previously in the performance.

When playing some of the slower beats such as the Bowra, try gradually reducing the volume and fading out to nothing - this can create an eerie atmosphere. Or for an exciting end to a performance have the entire group play round and round the African rhythm, gradually increasing the speed of the beat until it is too fast to play and then let the rhythm collapses into a long roll. The leader will then raise their hands and the group will stop playing. When the leader lowers their hands the group recommence the loud rolls. Alternate between long and short rolls and make sure everyone in the group is watching the leader as they may try and catch you out! To finish, the group follows the leader as they slowly play one hand after the other, gradually speeding up until the group plays one last long roll.

Chapter

9

Ten Tunes

First we'll show you how to set up a steady pulse. This will be a useful model for starting to learn all the African tunes in the book. The rest of this chapter comprises ten African tunes written out in grid music form as explained in Chapter 3.

Each African tune has accompanying Teaching and Learning notes to help explain the best way to learn and perform each one. When playing the tunes try to make sure that each rhythm is played hand-to-hand (R-L-R-L-etc) so you don't use just one hand all the time.

The music is arranged in order of difficulty with each new African rhythm introducing a fresh challenge.

When learning each African rhythm for the first time, begin with the easiest part, which I will identify in the Teaching and Learning notes for each tune. Make sure the group can play this part well with a good steady pulse before moving on to the next part. Ensure the whole group learns each part together before dividing up the group with each section playing their own part to create the whole tune.

Always practise the Call and Responses separately before joining them to the African rhythms. As with The Conga, try making up words and phrases to help you remember the rhythms.

Space has been left under each beat on the grid for you to add your own words.

Setting up a Simple Pulse

The first task when playing our African tunes is to establish a steady pulse. This is done in the following way. First ask the entire group to play the rhythm for Drums One with a Low, bass tone, played in the centre of the drum.

Count out loud 1-2-3-4- round and round, playing the Low bass tone only on beat number 1 as below.

Drums One (Large Djembe)

1	2	3	4	5	6	7	8	9	10	11	12	13	14	15	16
L	O	O	O	L	O	O	O	L	O	O	O	L	O	O	O

Low-rest-rest-rest   Low-rest-rest-rest-etc.

This will maintain a steady pulse. When this rhythm is established leave just two of the large drums to continue with the part for Drums One and begin to teach the rest of the group Drums Two. Drums Two plays two high or open tones on beats 1 and 2 and rests on beats 3 and 4 as below.

Drums Two (Medium Djembe)

1	2	3	4	5	6	7	8	9	10	11	12	13	14	15	16
H	H	O	O	H	H	O	O	H	H	O	O	H	H	O	O

High-high-rest-rest   High-high-rest-rest-etc.

This pattern is again repeated round and round. Wait until the group is comfortable playing both rhythms one and two together before rehearsing Drums Three. Drums Three rest on beats 1 and 2 then play a Low tone on beats 3 and 4.

Drums Three (Small Djembe)

1	2	3	4	5	6	7	8	9	10	11	12	13	14	15	16
O	O	L	L	O	O	L	L	O	O	L	L	O	O	L	L

Rest-rest-low-low   Rest-rest-low-low-etc.

Chapter 9

When the group can play each rhythm successfully as a whole, divide the drums into sections as described in Chapter 2 and practise playing all three rhythms simultaneously, as set out in the Full Score below, repeating round and round..

Drums One (Large Djembe)

1	2	3	4	5	6	7	8	9	10	11	12	13	14	15	16
L	O	O	O	L	O	O	O	L	O	O	O	L	O	O	O

Drums Two (Medium Djembe)

1	2	3	4	5	6	7	8	9	10	11	12	13	14	15	16
H	H	O	O	H	H	O	O	H	H	O	O	H	H	O	O

Drums Three (Small Djembe)

1	2	3	4	5	6	7	8	9	10	11	12	13	14	15	16
O	O	L	L	O	O	L	L	O	O	L	L	O	O	L	L

The Ten African Drumming tunes will now be presented using the grid music score.

All tunes in this book are graduated so that each new tune is slightly more advanced that the previous tune and introduces more musical challenges

Tune 1: SOGO

As was explained in the previous musical example, we first need to establish a steady pulse. Referring to the full score opposite, first ask the entire group to play the rhythm for Drums One, with a Low Bass tone in the centre of the drum. Count out loud 1-2-3-4- round and round playing the Low Bass tone only on beat number 1. i.e. Low-rest-rest-rest-Low-rest-rest-rest- etc.

When this rhythm is established leave just two of the larger drums to continue this and begin to teach the rest of the group the second rhythm for Drums Two. Drums Two plays a two bar rhythm. Drums Two rest on beats 1 and 2 then plays two high or open tones on beats 3 and 4, then rest on the following beats 5 and 6 then plays a low or Bass tone on beats 7 and 8 etc. i.e. rest-rest-High-High-rest-rest-Low-Low-etc.

This pattern is now repeated round and round. Wait until the group is comfortable playing rhythms one and two together before rehearsing the rhythm for Drums Three. Drums Three plays a two bar rhythm. The first half is played with a high tone on beat 1, a rest on beat 2, another high on beat 3 and a rest on beat 4. i.e. High-rest-High-rest-etc. Practise this first.

The second half of rhythm three plays a low tone on beats 5 and 6, rests on beat 7 and then plays a high tone on beat 8. i.e. Low-Low-rest-High-etc. When the group is able to play these two rhythms separately try to play them one after another so they fit together to complete the phrase. i.e. High-rest-High-rest-Low-Low-rest-High-etc.

This complete rhythm is now repeated round and round. As Drums Three play a two bar rhythm it may take a little more time to settle in.

To create a performance, begin with rhythm one and then build in rhythms two and three. When all three rhythms have been playing together for a while insert Call and Response 1B. After this, slip back into the tune with all three rhythms playing simultaneously round and round. End the performance by playing Call and Response 1B, twice.

For adding percussion to this tune you can use the Percussion Buddies example on page 26.

Audio Example
AD1-1-Sogo.mp3 full score

Sogo Full Score

Drums One (Large Djembe)

1	2	3	4	5	6	7	8	9	10	11	12	13	14	15	16
L	O	O	O	L	O	O	O	L	O	O	O	L	O	O	O

Drums Two (Medium Djembe)

1	2	3	4	5	6	7	8	9	10	11	12	13	14	15	16
O	O	H	H	O	O	L	L	O	O	H	H	O	O	L	L

Drums Three (Small Djembe)

1	2	3	4	5	6	7	8	9	10	11	12	13	14	15	16
H	O	H	O	L	L	O	H	H	O	H	O	L	L	O	H

Chapter

9

Tune 2: POLOLE

Begin with the entire group playing the part for Drums One with a Low Bass tone on beat numbers 1, 5, 9, 13 etc.
i.e. Low-rest-rest-rest-Low-rest-rest-rest-etc.
1 2 3 4 5 6 7 8

This will establish our pulse.

Leave two players to continue with the pulse of rhythm one while the rest of the group practises the rhythm for Drums Two.
Drums Two rest for beats 1 and 2 then play a Low tone on beats 3 and 4 then rest for the next beat 5, play a high tone on beats 6 and 7 then rest on beat 8 etc.
i.e. rest-rest-Low-Low-rest-High-High-rest-etc.
1 2 3 4 5 6 7 8
This pattern is now repeated round and round.

Wait until the group is comfortable playing rhythms one and two together before rehearsing Drums Three.
Drums Three play a high tone on beat 1, rest on beats 2 and 3 then play a high tone on beat 4, another high tone on the next beat 5, a rest on beat 6 and a Low tone on beats 7 and 8.
i.e. High-rest-rest-High-High-rest-Low-Low-etc.
1 2 3 4 5 6 7 8
This pattern is repeated round and round.

When the group can play all the rhythms individually divide up the group and play all the rhythms simultaneously.

To create a performance build in each rhythm separately. When all the rhythms are playing together gradually increase the tempo so the music becomes faster. When you have reached the maximum speed at which you can comfortably play the tune add in Call and Response 2A twice and then return to the tune at the fast tempo. Now gradually slow down the speed and fade out each rhythm at a time until only Drums One are left to fade away.

For adding percussion to this tune you can use the Percussion Buddies example on page 26.

Chapter

9

Audio Example
AD1-2-Polole..mp3 full score

Polole Full Score

Drums One (Large Djembe)

1	2	3	4	5	6	7	8	9	10	11	12	13	14	15	16
L	O	O	O	L	O	O	O	L	O	O	O	L	O	O	O

Drums Two (Medium Djembe)

1	2	3	4	5	6	7	8	9	10	11	12	13	14	15	16
O	O	L	L	O	H	H	O	O	O	L	L	O	H	H	O

Drums Three (Small Djembe)

1	2	3	4	5	6	7	8	9	10	11	12	13	14	15	16
H	O	O	H	H	O	L	L	H	O	O	H	H	O	L	L

Tune 3: KOUKOU

To establish the pulse practise the rhythm for Drums One with a high tone on beat 1 and rests on beats 2, 3 and 4 followed by a Low tone on the next beat 5 and rests on beats 6, 7 and 8 etc.
i.e. High-rest-rest-rest-Low-rest-rest-rest-etc.

1 2 3 4 5 6 7 8

Leave two players to continue playing Drums One and introduce Drums Two.

Drums Two play a two bar rhythm.

This begins with a high tone on beat 1, a rest on beat 2, a low tone on beats 3 and 4 with rests on the following beats 5 and 6, a high tone on beat 7 and a rest on beat 8 etc.

i.e. High-rest-Low-Low-rest-rest-High-rest-etc.

1 2 3 4 5 6 7 8

This pattern is repeated round and round. practise playing Drums One and two together before rehearsing Drums Three.

Drums Three introduce a four bar rhythm.

Drums Three play a low tone on beat 1, rest on beat 2, play a high tone on beat 3 and rest on beat 4 then repeat this sequence for the next four beats 5 to 8, next is a low tone on beat 9, a high tone on beat 10, a rest on beat 11 and a high tone on beat 12 before returning to a low tone on beat 13, a rest on beat 14, a high tone on beat 15 and a rest on beat 16.

i.e. Low-rest-High-rest-Low-rest-High-rest-Low-High-rest-High-Low-rest-High-rest-etc.

1 2 3 4 5 6 7 8 9 10 11 12 13 14 15 16

This is a longer rhythm so take your time to rehearse it thoroughly before practising playing all three rhythms together.

For adding percussion to this tune you can use the Percussion Buddies example on page 26.

Chapter

9

Audio Example
AD1-3-Koukou.mp3 full score

Koukou Full Score

Drums One (Large Djembe)

1	2	3	4	5	6	7	8	9	10	11	12	13	14	15	16
H	O	O	O	L	O	O	O	H	O	O	O	L	O	O	O

Drums Two (Medium Djembe)

1	2	3	4	5	6	7	8	9	10	11	12	13	14	15	16
H	O	L	L	O	O	H	O	H	O	L	L	O	O	H	O

Drums Three (Small Djembe)

1	2	3	4	5	6	7	8	9	10	11	12	13	14	15	16
L	O	H	O	L	O	H	O	L	H	O	H	L	O	H	O

Now is a good time to try joining tunes together in a performance.
The three tunes we have covered so far Sogo, Polole and Koukou are similar in style and will fit well together in an extended performance.

We can begin with Sogo and use Call and Response 1A as a bridge into Polole. Call and Response 1B can then lead us into Koukou. Try experimenting by mixing any combination of the tunes and linking them with the Call and Responses to create your own unique performance piece.

Tune 4: JONGO

The first rhythm to learn is for Drums One as this part simply repeats the same beat round and round.

i.e. Low-rest-High-High-Low-rest-High-High etc.

1 2 3 4 5 6 7 8

practise this until it can be played at a fairly fast tempo (around 120bpm - same as a clock ticking). When this can be played satisfactorily, begin to learn the parts for Drums Two and three, which will sound a if it's at half the speed of the rhythm of Drums One and has a longer repeated phrase.

i.e. Low-rest-rest-rest-High-rest-high-rest-Low-rest-rest-rest- High-High-High-High etc

1 2 3 4 5 6 7 8 9 10 11 12 13 14 15 16

Now begin to play both parts together, remembering that although the pulse remains the same, part two will sound slower than part one.

For adding percussion to this tune you can use the Percussion Buddies example on page 26.

Jongo Full Score

Audio Example
AD1-4-Jongo.mp3 full score

Drums One (Large Djembe)

1	2	3	4	5	6	7	8	9	10	11	12	13	14	15	16
L	O	H	H	L	O	H	H	L	O	H	H	L	O	H	H

Drums Two and Three (Medium and Small Djembe)

1	2	3	4	5	6	7	8	9	10	11	12	13	14	15	16
L	O	O	O	H	O	H	O	L	O	O	O	H	H	H	H

To create a performance start with drum part two only then add in part one. After playing round and round for a while add in Call and Response 1B and then go back to the tune with both parts coming in together. Again play round and round before ending with the Call and Response 1B played four times.

Chapter

9

Tune 5: BOWRA

Unlike some previous tunes, in Bowra, Drums One does not always have a repeated heavy low note on beat 1.

In this tune all three parts are made up of repeated two bar rhythms as follows.

Drums One:

i.e. Low-rest-High-rest-High-rest-High-rest-etc.

1 2 3 4 5 6 7 8

Drums Two:

i.e Low-rest-High-High-High-rest-Low-rest-etc.

1 2 3 4 5 6 7 8

Drums Three:

i.e Low-rest-rest-High-rest-rest-High-rest-etc.

1 2 3 4 5 6 7 8

As before, practise each rhythm separately with the whole group before playing all three rhythms simultaneously.

For adding percussion to this tune you can use the Percussion Buddies example on page 26.

Chapter 9

Bowra Full Score

Audio Example
AD1-5-Bowra.mp3 full score

Drums One (Large Djembe)

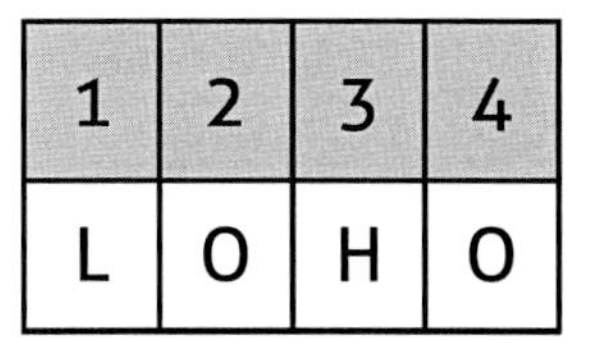

1	2	3	4	5	6	7	8	9	10	11	12	13	14	15	16
L	O	H	O	H	O	H	O	L	O	H	O	H	O	H	O

Drums Two (Medium Djembe)

1	2	3	4	5	6	7	8	9	10	11	12	13	14	15	16
L	O	H	H	H	O	L	O	L	O	H	H	H	O	L	O

Drums Three (Small Djembe)

1	2	3	4	5	6	7	8	9	10	11	12	13	14	15	16
L	O	O	H	O	O	H	O	L	O	O	H	O	O	H	O

To create a performance try swapping the parts around after a Call and Response with Drums One playing the Drums Two part and Drums Two playing the Drums Three part etc.

Tune 6: D'JOLE

The first rhythm to learn here is for Drums Two. This is because the bigger Drums playing rhythm one do not play at the beginning of the tune. This is an interesting feature of D'jole.

As we will need to establish a pulse we will begin by learning the rhythm for Drums Two.

This is a two bar rhythm.

i.e.High-rest-rest-High-High-rest-Low-Low-etc.

1 2 3 4 5 6 7 8

This is repeated round and round.

Next we will learn the rhythm for Drums Three.

This is a four bar rhythm.

i.e. rest-rest-High-High-rest-rest-Low-Low-rest-High-High-rest-rest-rest-Low-low-etc.

1 2 3 4 5 6 7 8 9 10 11 12 13 14 15 16

This is also repeated round and round.

Finally we add in Drums One, who play only two low notes in the middle of the tune on beats 9 and 12.

i.e. rest-rest-rest-rest-rest-rest-rest-rest-Low-rest-rest-Low-rest-rest-rest-rest-etc.

1 2 3 4 5 6 7 8 9 10 11 12 13 14 15 16

Although drums one only play two low notes on beats 9 and 12 these are very important and should be played with a loud accent.

For adding percussion to this tune you can use the Percussion Buddies example on page 26.

Chapter

9

D'Jole Full Score

Audio Example
/AD1-6-Djole.mp3.full score

Drums One (Large Djembe)

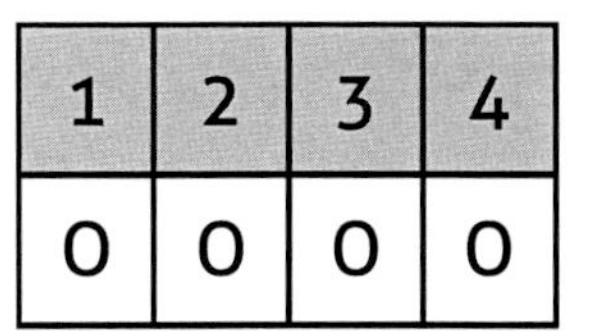

1	2	3	4
O	O	O	O

5	6	7	8
O	O	O	O

9	10	11	12
L	O	O	L

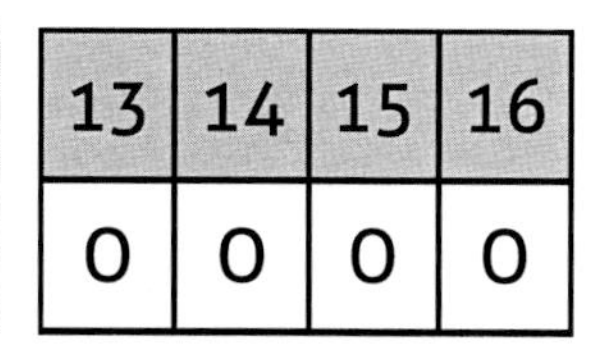

13	14	15	16
O	O	O	O

Drums Two (Medium Djembe)

1	2	3	4
H	O	O	H

5	6	7	8
H	O	L	L

9	10	11	12
H	O	O	H

13	14	15	16
H	O	L	L

Drums Three (Small Djembe)

1	2	3	4
O	O	H	H

5	6	7	8
O	O	L	L

9	10	11	12
O	H	H	O

13	14	15	16
O	O	L	L

The Bowra and D'jole work well together as a joint performance piece.
Try linking them together with Call and Response 1B.

Chapter

9

Tune 7: MADAGASCAR

This tune is in 6/8 time. This means that there are six beats in each bar instead of the usual four in the previous pieces. You will notice that the music also has a different feel with a laid back swing.

Drums One play a repeated rhythm of four high tones and two low tones.
i.e. High-High-High-High-Low-Low-High High-High-High-Low-Low

1 2 3 4 5 6 1 2 3 4 5 6 etc.

Drums Two and three play a high tone on beat 1, rest on beats 2 and 3 two high tones on beats 4 and five and rest on beat 6 then follow on with a rest on the next beat 1, two high tones on beats 2 and 3 a rest on beat 4 and two low tones on beats 5 and 6.
i.e. High-rest-rest-High-High-rest-rest-High-High-rest-Low-Low-etc.

1 2 3 4 5 6 1 2 3 4 5 6

This rhythm is also repeated round and round.

Be sure to practise each rhythm individually before playing them together.

To add an extra dimension to performances try introducing moments of silence in the middle of the tune. For example play round the tune a few times and then on a signal from the leader everyone should stop playing and count six beats rest before resuming with the tune. As the group becomes confident with this, increase the duration of the rests to 12 or 24 beats silence.

You can use the same approach in any tune, but count rests of just 4, 8 and 12 beats in the tunes with a 4 beat pulse.

For adding percussion to this tune you can use the Percussion Buddies example on page 29.

Chapter

9

Audio Example
AD1-7-Madagascar.mp3 full score

Madagascar Full Score

Drums One (Large Djembe)

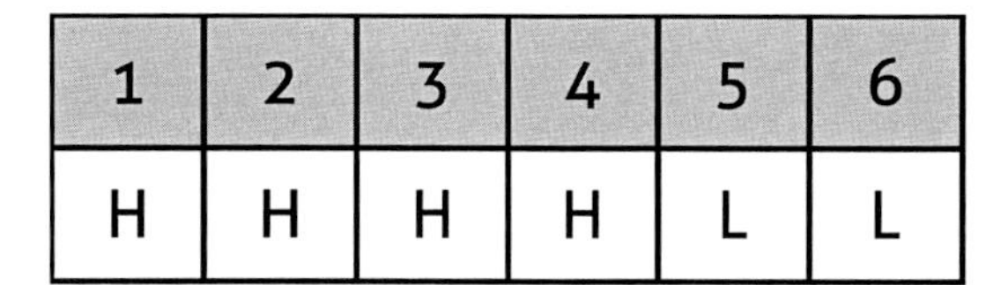

1	2	3	4	5	6
H	H	H	H	L	L

1	2	3	4	5	6
H	H	H	H	L	L

Drums Two (Medium Djembe)

1	2	3	4	5	6
H	O	O	H	H	O

1	2	3	4	5	6
O	H	H	O	L	L

Drums Three (Small Djembe)

1	2	3	4	5	6
H	O	O	H	H	O

1	2	3	4	5	6
O	H	H	O	L	L

Chapter

9

Tune 8: M'BABA

M'baba is also in 6/8 time but has three separate rhythms and, like Koukou, Drums One will give us a steady pulse, but in this case remembering to count up to six.

Drums One plays a low tone on beat 1 and rests on beats 2, 3, 4, 5 and 6 followed by a high tone on the next beat 1 with rests on beats 2, 3, 4, 5 and 6.
i.e. Low-rest-rest-rest-rest-rest-High-rest-rest-rest-rest-rest-etc.

1 2 3 4 5 6 1 2 3 4 5 6

This rhythm is repeated round and round.
Drums Two play a one bar phrase of a high tone on beat 1, a rest on beat 2, three high tones on beats 3, 4 and five with a rest on beat 6.
i.e. Low-rest-High-High-High-rest-etc.

1 2 3 4 5 6

This rhythm is repeated round and round.

Now practise the rhythms for Drums One and two together.

Drums Three play a two bar phrase with a low tone on beat 1, rests on beats 2 and 3 a low tone on beat 4, a high tone on beat 5 and a rest on beat 6 followed by a low tone on the next beat 1, a rest on beat 2, three high tones on beats 3, 4 and 5 with a rest on beat 6.
i.e. Low-rest-rest-Low-High-rest-Low-rest-High-High-High-rest-etc.

1 2 3 4 5 6 1 2 3 4 5 6

This rhythm is also repeated round and round.

Add character to your performances by making changes in volume (dynamics) for dramatic effect. For example, play the first six beats of the three drum parts at a loud full volume and the second six beats of each part softly. Try experimenting with changes in volume in your music.

For adding percussion to this tune you can use the Percussion Buddies example on page 28.

Chapter

9

Audio Example
/AD1-8-M'baba.mp3full score

M'baba Full Score

Drums One (Large Djembe)

1	2	3	4	5	6
L	O	O	O	O	O

1	2	3	4	5	6
H	O	O	O	O	O

Drums Two (Medium Djembe)

1	2	3	4	5	6
L	O	H	H	H	O

1	2	3	4	5	6
L	O	H	H	H	O

Drums Three (Small Djembe)

1	2	3	4	5	6
L	O	O	L	H	O

1	2	3	4	5	6
L	O	H	H	H	O

Tune 9: THE CONGA

The teaching and learning notes for The Conga are incorporated into the weekly lessons in Chapter Seven.

Audio Example
AD1-9-The-Conga.mp3 full score

Drums One (Large Djembe)

1	2	3	4	5	6	7	8	9	10	11	12	13	14	15	16
L	L	L	L	O	O	O	O	L	L	L	L	O	O	O	O

Drums Two (Medium Djembe)

1	2	3	4	5	6	7	8	9	10	11	12	13	14	15	16
O	O	O	O	H	OH	O	O	O	O	O	O	H	OH	O	O

Drums Three (Small Djembe)

1	2	3	4	5	6	7	8	9	10	11	12	13	14	15	16
O	O	O	O	H	OH	O	O	O	O	O	O	H	OH	O	O

You will notice that on beats 6 and 14 the cell contains both a rest and a high sound. This is to indicate that this high sound, which makes up the ga part of conga, is to be played on the second half of that beat, this is sometimes known to as an "off beat". Please listen to The Conga mp3 track to see how this should sound.

For adding percussion to this tune you can use the Percussion Buddies example on page 30.

Chapter 9

Tune 10 : FANGA

Begin with the entire group learning the rhythm for Drums One.
This is a simple repeated rhythm.
i.e. Low-rest-High-High-Low-rest-High-High-etc.

1 2 3 4 1 2 3 4

Once this is established, leave two of the large drums to continue this rhythm and teach the rest of the group Drums Two.
This is a four bar rhythm.
i.e. Low-rest-rest-High-rest-High-High-rest-Low-rest-Low-rest-High-High-rest-rest-etc.

1 2 3 4 5 6 7 8 9 10 11 12 13 14 15 16

Continue with the large drums playing Drums One and the medium drums playing part two while you teach the small drums part three.
This is also a four bar rhythm.
i.e. Low-rest-rest-Low-rest-rest-High-High-Low-rest-rest-Low-Low-rest-High-High-etc.

1 2 3 4 5 6 7 8 9 10 11 12 13 14 15 16

Now practise playing all three rhythms simultaneously.

For adding percussion to this tune you can use the Percussion Buddies example on page 26.

Audio Example
AD1-10-Fanga.mp3 full score

The Fanga Full Score

Drums One (Large Djembe)

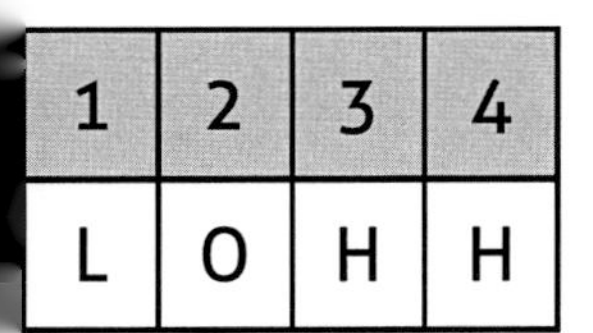

1	2	3	4	5	6	7	8	9	10	11	12	13	14	15	16
L	O	H	H	L	O	H	H	L	O	H	H	L	O	H	H

Drums Two (Medium Djembe)

1	2	3	4	5	6	7	8	9	10	11	12	13	14	15	16
L	O	O	H	O	H	H	O	L	O	L	O	H	H	O	O

Drums Three (Small Djembe)

1	2	3	4	5	6	7	8	9	10	11	12	13	14	15	16
L	O	O	L	O	O	H	H	L	O	O	L	L	O	H	H

When you have mastered all the African tunes in the book experiment with linking them together with the Call and Responses. Try improvising your own rhythms around the tunes and enjoy making your performances interesting and diverse by employing all the elements of music.